G000153723

A BOOT UP

THE SOUTH WEST COAST PATH

SOUTH DEVON

Philip Carter

First published in Great Britain in 2010

British Library Cataloguing-in-Publication Data
A CIP record for this title is available from the British Library

ISBN 978 0 85710 012 2

PiXZ Books
Halsgrove House, Ryelands Industrial Estate,
Bagley Road, Wellington, Somerset TA21 9PZ
Tel: 01823 653777
Fax: 01823 216796
email: sales@halsgrove.com

An imprint of Halstar Ltd, part of the Halsgrove group of companies
Information on all Halsgrove titles is available at: www.halsgrove.com

Printed and bound in China by Toppan Leefung Printing Ltd

Contents

The South West Coast Path – South Devon

How to use this book

The South West Coast Path offers all things to all people. For those who require a real challenge there are 630 miles (1014 km) of continuous path some of it rugged indeed. However, other parts are entirely flat and make for the easiest of walking. Whatever your choice it is hoped that this little selection will give you pleasure and maybe items of interest as well. The 'level' shown near the beginning of each walk is an indication of the exertion required. 🌺 🌺 🌺 will take more effort than 🌺 🌺 and 🌺 🌺 than 🌺 .

The waymark for the Coast Path, as it is indeed for all official long distance trails or footpaths, is a single upright acorn. So if you are in doubt as to whether you are on or off the path - look for the acorn. Having said that be careful as the National Trust use a spray of acorns as a symbol and some of the Coast Path belongs to them. Therefore you can find stretches with both. But as stated at the outset if you see a single upright acorn you are on the Coast Path.

In this series there is a selection of short, mostly circular walks, taking in parts of the Coast Path. Because they are mostly circular they can of course be walked in reverse. However, they are devised to provide the best views so it is suggested you try them first as described. To give more opportunities of access and to vary the terrain and experience the walks chosen are spread along the coast. The one thing that they all have in common is a high scenic value. None of them are dull and many incorporate short stretches of the best the Coast Path has to offer.

Remember too the origin of this Coastal Path was as a walking route for revenue men patrolling to prevent smuggling. This meant that the path had to hug the coastline. The revenue men had to be able to see the end of every headland and look into each creek and inlet.

Some walks pass places of refreshment others do not. But you are always well advised to carry a flask and a little something to eat. The views are never quite so good if you are hungry!

Undoubtedly the very best time to walk is the late spring when the coastal flowers are at their best. Having said that more people walk in summer than any other time and some walks are best when the autumn colours are in evidence. Go well shod with footwear that has a grip as this will make even the hardest walk easier.

Whatever time you pick to walk and whatever area you choose you can be assured there will always be something of interest to engage the mind. The coast has for centuries been a working place and old mills, fish cellars and limekilns bear this out. The coastline too has often in times of conflict been our first line of defence so much remains to remind you of wars in the past.

These walks provide a taste of what the Coast Path has to offer. If you get hooked the best source of further information is The South West Coast Path Association. They publish an updated annual guide as well as a set of Path Descriptions covering the whole path. They are also happy to answer specific enquiries. Contact the South West Coast Path Association (Registered Charity Number 266754) Bowker House, Lee Mill Bridge, Ivybridge, Devon, PL21 9EF
Telephone: 01752 896237
Fax: 01752 893654
E-mail info@swcp.org.uk
Web site www.swcp.org.uk

South Devon can deceive because of the big resorts such as Torquay, Paignton, Exmouth and the large city of Plymouth there is a tendency to regard it as all urban. This is far from being the case as some of the walks are remote and certainly most attractive.

Key to Symbols Used

Level of difficulty:

Easy 🍃

Fair 🍃 🍃

More challenging 🍃 🍃 🍃

Map symbols:

🚗 Park & start

—— Tarred Road

- - - - Footpath

■ Building / Town

+ Church

🍺 Pub

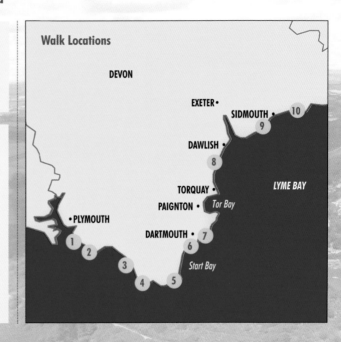

Walk Locations

DEVON

EXETER •

SIDMOUTH •

9

10

DAWLISH •

8

TORQUAY •

PAIGNTON •

Tor Bay

LYME BAY

• PLYMOUTH

DARTMOUTH •

7

6

Start Bay

1

2

3

4

5

1 Wembury – Warren Point

A short walk with superb views, taking in a Rocket House, and the famous Mew Stone.

This short walk although close to a heavily populated area has much to commend it. There are interesting views both of the sea and the River Yealm estuary (the River Yealm is pronounced Yam).

There is a long climb going inland but the rest of the walk is easier.

Level 🥾🥾
Length just under four and a half miles (7.2 km.)
Park at National Trust car park at Wembury 519 484
OS Map Explorer OL20 South Devon
Refreshments teashop in Old Mill below car park.

The Mewstone.

① From the car park below the church go down towards the beach, passing the Old Mill, noting the Mewstone out to sea. Turn right and soon cross a little wooden bridge. There turn immediately right on to a path through a field. This is signposted 'Lynmouth 117 miles' and has a Coast to Coast waymark. [Your route from seashore until you reach the third road is both 'Coast to Coast' and 'Erme–Plym Trail']. Walk

Rock samphire near Old Mill Café.

The church may have been positioned where it acts as a daymark for shipping. It is dedicated to St Werburgh and has connections with the founding of Western Australia. A local family, the Lockyers, provided the commander of the Brig Amity that planted the first settlement at Albany in 1826. The novelist John Galsworthy used this area of Devon as the setting in Swan Song when Soames Forsyte returns to the home of his ancestors. Galsworthy himself had visited in 1912. The Mewstone, surprising as it may seem, was inhabited for a number of years. One of the last occupants was a certain Sam Wakeham, a warrener whose tenure on the islet was cut short when his sideline in smuggling was discovered! Later it became Ministry of Defence property and is now a nature reserve. Mew is an old word for seagull so mewstone merely means gull rock. Opposite the Old Mill look for rock samphire, mentioned in Shakespeare's King Lear and once eaten pickled. Train Road has nothing to do with railways but derives from the fact that 'trains' of laden donkeys taking sand and seaweed (used as fertiliser) from the beach used that route.

A distant view of Wembury Point.

want. You come to a stile, cross it and bear right. At the next road turn left for a short distance downhill to turn right on the continuation of the trail. This is signposted 'Public footpath Train Road ½ mile'. The track passes a house and narrows to a footpath. There is then a long ascent, two footpaths join from the left but ignore these. The path crosses the middle of two large fields. At the top of the second the path swings right and down through another field to come to a third road. Here you leave the trail by turning right. Take the first left, a narrow road between walls. The road takes a right angle, turn up a slope to come up to the main road. There is a convenience store here if it is hot and you want a cool drink!

up the field and cross another bridge. The path then bears slightly right to go up a slope towards a rail fence and gate. Exit through the gate, turn left and cross the main road. The path you want is opposite and signed 'Bridleway No 20' it is concrete at the start then forks left and becomes a muddy track. You come to a three way junction, the centre one signed 'Coast to Coast' and 'Erme Plym Trail' is the one you

2 Cross the main road with care to the footpath opposite. This is at first enclosed, at the T-junction turn left. After a few yards the path turns right up steps signed 'Allotments'. Cross a field passing through the allotments to come to kissing gates by a wall. Later the wall gets higher and this is the back wall of Wembury House. Go forward via a kissing gate and steps to the road. Here bear right and walk down the road which passes through a gate signed 'Link to Coastpath' The road becomes a track, stay with it, down to the Rocket House, ignoring a path going left.

Wembury House was built in 1830 for the Lockyer family. One later member became a lord-mayor of Plymouth

The Mewstone at sunset.

and there is still a street in that town with the family name. There is a high level promenade behind the high wall so do not be surprised if you see someone looking down on you! The Rocket House was of course originally where rockets were stored for use in rescues from shipwrecks. The inventor of the rocket life-saving device was Henry Trengrouse. His invention was to save thousands of lives yet his financial reward from the government was so small that he died in complete poverty!

3 At the Rocket House go through the gate and turn right on the Coast Path. You soon have splendid views of the Yealm and walk past some Monterey Pines. There is an unsigned junction the true Coast Path is the left fork with the better views. Look out to sea for good views of the Mewstone and, if visibility is good, the Eddystone Lighthouse. The

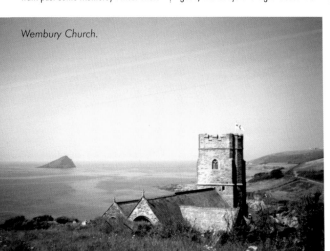

Wembury Church.

Beyond the Rocket House look for Mugwort the leaves of which were once dried and used by Cornish miners as a substitute for tea.

right fork will take you to the same place more quickly but is less scenic. Continue following the Coast Path signs - there is one unsigned junction by a small wall. Here bear left avoiding path going into a field. Later there is a left turn signed 'Link to Coastpath' ignore this as you are

Monterey Pines overlook the Yealm estuary.

already on it! The Coast Path continues down close to the church to reach the car park, by Wembury Marine Centre. Wembury Marine Centre as it advertises itself shows you a 'world beneath the waves'. Monterey Pines seen here are originally from California.

The present Eddystone Lighthouse is the fourth. The first was Winstanley's, made of wood, and completed in 1698, it was swept away along with its builder in a mighty storm. The second, Rudyard's in 1705, also of wood, burnt down. The third, Smeaton's in 1759, and the first of stone, was undermined by the sea; so it was taken down except for the stump and re-erected on Plymouth Hoe; The fourth to be erected on the Eddystone, 10 miles offshore, Douglas's in 1882, also of stone, survives today. This was automated a hundred years later in 1982.

2 Noss Mayo

A light and relatively easy walk along a former carriage drive and with views of coastal villages.

The major part of this walk makes use of Lady Baring's carriage drive a well-engineered scenic route above the sea and overlooking the estuary of the Yealm. After the hill at the start this is a very easy walk.

Level 🐾 🐾 one longish hill at the start but then the majority is the easiest of walking.

Length about four and a half miles (7.2 km.)

Park at Noss Mayo in the car park next to the tennis courts 546 473

OS Map Explorer OL20 South Devon

Refreshments at the two pubs in Noss Mayo and there is a tea room nearby in Newton Ferrers open Wednesday to Sunday.

Newton Creek.

1 Exit the car park turning left up the road that deteriorates into a stony lane. At the top of the hill you join a metalled road turn left but very shortly right along a footpath, signed 'link to Coast Path'. There is a National Trust car park next to the footpath. The footpath leads down to a stile, go over it to follow the track bearing right. In a short while you join Lady Baring's carriage drive.

Lady Baring's carriage drive.

Newton Ferrers and Noss Mayo are shortened by locals to simply Newton and Noss. Noss is the equivalent of ness, a headland, belonging to Mayo (an early variation of Matthew). The carriage drive was constructed at the behest of Lord Revelstoke a member of the Baring banking family who lived at nearby Membland Hall. Guests were driven round the drive and servants were despatched to the other end to prepare tea for the guests' arrival!

2 This is the Coast Path, keep right. Then simply follow the well graded easy walking of the carriage drive it is waymarked with acorns, ignoring all side paths. You pass Warren Cottage and later the path turns significantly right at the mouth of the Yealm. Behind the second length of wall on your left is a

Newton Ferrers and the River Yealm.

Ferry charges shown on an tariff board.

TOLLS DUE and PAYABLE TO YEALM FERRY
Ferriage for each Person on Week Days
The Like On Sundays
Ferriage for every Pony or Ass
Dº for every Bag Corn or Potatoes
Anchorage for every Vessel
Ballasting for Ditto

Go ahead for a few yards and at a small parking bay there is a footpath slightly to the right going up a slope, take this. There is a National Trust sign saying 'Ferry Wood'. Walk

seat with a wonderful view. The path goes through a wood passing a housing terrace on the right which was the one time coastguard row. You pass a large building with a small spire, the last part is called Battery Cottage, the name is on the house wall but you have to look for it. The path starts to

descend and shortly by an information board 'Passage Wood' the path leaves the carriage drive going down steps left. This path dips to the old ferry point, with its tariff board on the right; look for this. The path, now a track, rises slightly to rejoin the drive just after a letter box in a brick pillar.

Warren Cottage is so called because it was the home of the Warrener who farmed rabbits. • If conditions are good Eddystone Lighthouse can be seen out to sea. • Coastguard Cottages are a reminder of why the Coast Path came into existence in the first place. • There was once a gun battery site at Battery Cottage. • A folk name for Wall Valerian is 'Drunkards' because they sway in the slightest breeze.

through the woods passing above the new ferry landing point.

3 At the end you come down the steps to join the drive where you go right. Continue along the road through Noss Mayo; ignore all turnings off and proceed up a slope. At the top bear right to the car park beside the tennis courts.

Newton Ferrers and Noss Mayo are joined by a footpath across Newton Creek at low tide. Noss Mayo was granted a market in 1286 but that has long since ceased. Not all that long ago there were two shops here at the point you enter but you would have a job to pinpoint them now after conversions. One used to have an old fashioned baker's peel, a wooden shovel for taking loaves out of a deep oven, hanging from the ceiling.

Newton Ferrers.

Wall Valerian and view across Yealm.

3 **Bolt Tail**

Everything you would Hope to find, and Iron Age fort.

Many argue over which are the best bits of the South West Coast Path; this walk certainly takes in part of a section that rates very highly.

It has also, much of interest to engage the walker.

This walk has a low-key start but then simply gets better and better. It goes inland, descends to Hope then ascends back to Bolberry Down, taking in spectacular Bolt Tail.

Level 🥾🥾 the last part of the walk is nearly all uphill but there are superb views to compensate.
Length five and a half miles (8.8 km.)
Start National Trust Car Park Bolberry Down 690 384
OS Map Explorer OL20 South Devon
Refreshments at Bolberry Down and by a short diversion at Hope Cove.

Hope Cove

1000 m

① Walk back out of the car park to rise a little and then to go steeply down the road you have used to reach the car park. At the bottom at the road junction go briefly left and then fork right on the unsigned little road.

Long ago there were attempts at copper mining nearby but these failed. • The Port Light Hotel was built as a golf club house in 1909 but fell out of use before World War I. • The wireless mast is to aid navigation.

② Walk past a massive farmyard and through the tiny hamlet of Bolberry and up the hill the other side. As you ascend there is a small

lane going left, take this. It is nicely signed 'Sweetheart's Lane' and more mundanely 'Galmpton'. At the T-junction turn left, 'Public Footpath', shortly passing by a gate 'Higher Barton', and just before the next gate turn right up a footpath which passes

besides an orchard. It then climbs diagonally through a small field swinging right to go up a bigger field to get to the top of the rise. At the summit pass through a big gate and immediately turn left through another gate.

Fishing boats at Hope Cove.

A barton is usually a big farm but the origin of the word is interesting. In the Middle Ages the lords of the manor would tenant the poorer land but keep the best land for their home farm. The best land would be able to grow barley, hence the name 'bar-ton'.

Coastguard Row at Hope.

3 As soon as you go through the gate look right to see Galmpton Church and later Burgh Island. The path descends slowly through several large fields to join a road on the outskirts of Hope. Shortly you cross a main road to go down steps besides another church, St Clements.

The church seen to the north is the new church of Galmpton replacing one at South Huish which had fallen into disrepair. The site was given by the Earl of Devon whose family were once large landowners in this area. The hotel on Burgh Island entertained not only Agatha Christie but also Edward VIII (when Prince of Wales) who stayed with Wallis Simpson.

Inner Hope.

(4) At the bottom of the slope you join the Coast Path. This is decision time, if you want refreshment turn right for Outer Hope, if you have brought your own turn left to continue the walk, shortly rejoining and going ahead on the main road.

Just before the old lifeboat house turn left and take the first right to see the attractive square of Inner Hope.

Retrace your steps to the lifeboat house and pass in front of it on the Coast Path.

There was once rivalry between the two Hopes. Outer Hopers versus Inner Hopers - but not no hopers! The hamlet was first recorded in the 13th century. The old lifeboat house was built in 1875 but operations were later transferred to South Sands at Salcombe. The terrace of cottages was formerly all a coastguard row. Surprising as it may seem there was once a cinema in Inner Hope - it was called The Barn - because it had been just that previously! It is reported that a large spider going across the screen could cause as much excitement as the film itself!

(5) The Coast Path climbs through a small wood, it then opens up dips into a valley and ascends again. Follow the sign forward for Bolt Tail looking right to see Thurlestone natural arch. Presently there is a right-forking unsigned grass path this will get you out to the Tail more quickly. In any case go to the rocky end for superb views down to the sea and along the coast, usually as far as Rame Head and exceptionally much further into Cornwall.

Thurlestone derives its name from the arch. In Old English 'thirled' described a holed stone, this surely means the arch has been there a very long time.

(6) Swing left and follow cliff top to leave the fortress high above but close to the sea. The path then ascends again slightly away from the cliff edge. After the second hump you are again closer to the sea and pass Ramilles Cove. The path dips and you pass through a gate.

Bolt Tail is a classic example of an Iron Age promontory fort c.2000 years old. • Ramilles Cove just beyond recalls the wreck at night in a gale of a warship of that name in 1760. Only 26 survived out of a crew of 734.

Thurlestone natural arch.

(7) There is a long steady climb but the views inland to Dartmoor and out to sea are more than compensation. At the top there is another gate and you walk along the heathland of Bolberry Down. Presently there is a fork, the right hand gives the better views. Look forward to see the Ham Stone out to sea. The path turns inland to regain the car park.

Bolberry Down was the site of one of the very early Radar Stations in World War II. • The Ham Stone was the scene in 1936 of the last English wreck of a clipper ship the Herzogin Cecilie.

Sunrise from Bolberry Down.

4 **Bolt Head**

A short walk to the site of a famous shipwreck

This is only a short walk but those who undertake it are unlikely to be disappointed.

A long climb at the start but you are soon rewarded with some outstanding views.

(1) Walk up the hill passing the entrance to Overbecks the path winds a little then swings right. Just as the slope eases there are steps going up left, take these. There follows a splendid high level walk to a direction indicator at Sharp Tor. Stop at this good viewpoint.

Fir Wood
3
Starehole Bottom
Off Cove
Bellhouse Rock
4
Bolt Head
Mew Stone
Little Mew Stone
2
1

1000 m

Level 🌂 🌂
Length under four miles (6.4 km.) but it is not a walk to be hurried.
Park at National Trust car park Overbecks, Salcombe 730 373, the crafty trick is to park at the bottom of the drive then you get the steepest hill first not last!
OS Map Explorer OL20 South Devon
Refreshments at N.T. Overbecks in season also near by at North Sands, Salcombe.

Salcombe Bar

Overbecks, an Edwardian house, was the home of Otto Overbecks from 1928 to 1937. A scientist and inventor, his collection was formed into a museum at the house. Now a National Trust property it has a superb exotic garden well worth a visit. • Sharp Tor is just over 400 feet high and an exceptional viewpoint.

(2) The path goes right and starts to descend, ignore path going right, signposted 'Soar Mill Cove 3 m', continue down hill. Cross a stream by a stone bridge and come out into a field. Go up a short distance diagonally to the right to come to a

Starehole Bay.

pedestrian gate, follow a distinct grass path through two fields. In the second field there is some rough ground then

a prominent white rock, keep right of it. Pass through another gate.

3 Here turn left, signposted 'Bolt Head ½' m, down the slope to pick up the Coast path to go around Bolt Head. The only place you might go wrong is where two footpaths meet just before the Head.

Here the more scenic route is bearing right down a wide gully signposted 'Salcombe 2¾' not the one signposted 'Salcombe 2½'. Descend the gully forking left behind Bolt Head.

Bolt Head was the site of a World War II look-out, part of which remains. Not the most clement of postings in winter one imagines!

Fort Charles or Salcombe Castle.

Herzogin Cecilie.
Opposite: Capstan of Herzogin Cecilie.

4 Shortly stop at the stone seat for another wonderful view. Drop down to Starehole Bay, ignore the path going left inland. The next section is a dramatic rock-cut stretch called the Courtenay Walk. Then follow the Coast Path back to 'Overbecks' car park.

Starehole Bay is the resting place of the Herzogin Cecilie the last clipper ship to be wrecked in England, in 1936. After grounding on the Ham Stone off Soar Mill Cove she was towed into Salcombe, but then when hopes of repair were abandoned she was brought out here to sink. • The Courtenay Walk was cut at the behest of the Courtenay family whose seat was then at Powderham on the Exe estuary. They were one of the biggest landowners in Devon with extensive holdings here in the South Hams district. • The well known Salcombe Bar, inspiration for Tennyson's poem 'Crossing the Bar' extends across the entrance to the estuary.

5 Start Point – Hallsands

Devon's most southerly point and a vanished village.

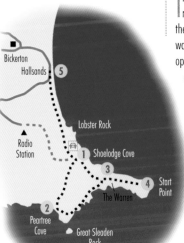

It takes a while to get to this remote corner of South Devon but the reward is in the walking. If you want to visit the lighthouse check the opening times put up on the big gate at the car park.

This walk is only circular in part so you do have sometimes to retrace your steps. However, the walking and indeed interest is such that you are unlikely to have regrets. The distance given above does include the option of going right to the lighthouse.

Level 💚 💚
Length under four miles (6.4 km)
Park at car park for Start Point 821 385.
OS Map Explorer OL20 South Devon
Refreshments an ice cream van sometimes operates in the car park but you will be wise to take your own fare.

Start Point.

| 1000 m |

Start Point.

1 From your car walk to the large gate at the south-west corner of the car park, this is in fact the continuation of the road to the lighthouse. Immediately after the gate a footpath, signed 'Great Mattiscombe Sand' goes right, take this. It goes downhill to above Mattiscombe Beach to join the Coast Path. Here go forward signed 'Start Point'. Look right for views along the coast to Prawle Point. Very soon by a wooden bench seat there is a path down to the beach for those wanting a swim!

2 Walkers bear left to dip and rise on the Coast Path then to dip again to go round Peartree Point. A place to pause and admire the view especially dramatic when the seas are high. There is then a long climb to the ridge, rocky in places at first, but then easy. There are good views forward to Start Point lighthouse. At the top of the ridge the sweep of Start Bay comes into view. Go over the ridge bearing left shortly down to the lighthouse road. Note the Coast Path sign as you join the road.

(3) Some folk will then wish to take the option of turning right to get a closer view of the

Worked stones dating from the Stone Age have been found at Peartree Point. • Grey Seals with their white pups can sometimes be seen on the off shore islets. • The ridge with sharp points you have crossed is made from metamorphic (changed by heat) rocks and was once described as being like the back of a dinosaur! • Foxgloves grow here, folk names include Fairy Bells and Witches' Gloves. • The Coast Path sign shows you, either way, just how far you can walk should you be so inclined.

lighthouse. But if lighthouses do not interest or the feet are weary you can turn left.

Apple arch across the path.

Peartree Point.

'Start' is the old English word for tail; we still use it in the name of the bird Redstart. • Henry Mugg, a pirate, was hanged here in chains as a warning to others in 1581. • The lighthouse was built in 1836 and automated in 1993. It is sometimes open to visitors. • Offshore are rocks called the Skerries one of the only two Norse names in Devon, the other being Lundy.

4 At the lighthouse about turn and walk up the road to the big gate Number 1. If it is a sunny summer day look for lizards on the wall beside the road and in any case there are the good views forward of Start Bay.

1 (again) Go over the stone stile by the gate and go ahead, signed 'Hallsands' on the grass path across the side of the car park. There is a slight dip before the path rises but then goes on a long decline passing at one point through a wood of cherry trees. At the bottom you are just above the old village of Hallsands which you can see by turning right from a viewing platform.

Start Point from the cherry wood.

The ruins at Old Hallsands.

The cherry wood, the only one on the Coast Path is something of a mystery. Many of the trees appear a similar age so an accidental origin is unlikely. If they were planted why? Fruit, veneer for fine furniture or for pipes? • Old Hallsands a fishing village with a pub The London Inn had to be abandoned during a storm in the night in 1917. Dredging at sea, for the Devonport Dockyard, had lowered the beach which protected it from the sea.

5 It is then about turn again to ascend the hill back to the car park.

6 Dartmouth, Little Dartmouth

Cross a bridge over the Atlantic to Deadman's Cove.

This is the first of two walks close to Dartmouth. Until the rise of Plymouth, Dartmouth used to be the most important port in this area and therefore has a lot of historical interest as well as a wonderfully scenic setting.

This is a short walk and very rewarding with a lot of splendid views but it does have some rough paths and a steep climb.

Mouth of the Dart, and The Mewstone.

Level 🥾🥾 mostly easy but one fierce climb.
Length three and a half miles (5.6 km.)
Park at National Trust car park Little Dartmouth 874 492.
OS Map Explorer OL20 South Devon
Refreshments none unless you divert part way round to Dartmouth Castle.

Dartmouth, Little Dartmouth

(1) Walk along the bridleway eastwards, only signposted unhelpfully 'Public Bridleway'. If you are in the part of the car park nearest the sea this means turning right. Go through the former Little Dartmouth farm to arrive on tarmac behind the old Coastguard Row. Shortly stop by a seat to look across the river to Kingswear Castle and the daymark on the hilltop. Go down the hill to turn right on the Coast Path. Should you require sustenance then do not immediately turn right but go ahead

The old Coastguard Row is evidence that the Coast Path was originally a working footpath for patrolling revenue men.

following the Coast Path signs to the café by Dartmouth Castle. But if you do this you will need to come back uphill!

(2) There is then a long descent, take care at the end to keep to the left-hand path. There is a short cut going right but views are poorer. The path comes out just above the sea and you can proceed along to cross a bridge over the 'Atlantic'.

Once you get down close to the sea look for the wild cabbage, it grows in profusion here.

Blackstone Point had a battery in the seventeenth century. Our Scottish

neighbours like to get excited about their 'bridge over the Atlantic', here we have the same thing but Devonians are more relaxed about it!

(3) You climb steps and turn right over a stile (if you go ahead for a few yards from the stile you can look down into Compass Cove). Having turned right there is a steep slope and about half way up this the path goes off left. Paths will come in from right - ignore them.

From Compass Cove in 1860 one of the first submarine cables was laid to Guernsey.

Bridge over the 'Atlantic' near Dartmouth.

View from Coombe Point.

4 Presently the path goes sharply left, down past a pond and out towards Combe Point, there are several variations of path here but all will get you there. Just before Combe Point there is a large gate, here the path goes right. (However, many opt first to go left out on to Combe Point for the splendid view across the mouth of the river Dart.)

5 Continuing westwards along a grassy route, towards Warren Cove, the path turns right. Half way up the slope a narrow path goes left through gorse, this is narrower but gives better views. If you miss it, it does not matter; at the top you have to turn left and come out at the same point below a gate. As you climb look for the tower of Stoke Fleming church.

The word 'warren' reminds us they would have farmed rabbits near here in time gone by. However, in case you are worried, the offshore rocks called the Dancing Bears do not betoken any of those animals in the vicinity! Stoke Fleming church was probably built where it is as daymark for shipping, like Wembury. At the church is buried Elias Newcomen great grandfather of Thomas Newcomen 1663-1729. It was Thomas who invented the first steam engine. These were mainly used for pumping water out of mines. James Watt who often gets credit for inventing steam engines was not born until after Newcomen had died.

6 The path then simply goes inland along three field edges until you reach the car park.

It may surprise you to know that the lower part of the car park used to be a tennis court.

The Countryside Commission claimed the piece of coast hereabouts was entirely unsuitable for a coastal path. Be your own judge as to whether they were correct in their thinking. The Devon Women's Institute to commemorate their Golden Jubilee in 1970 happily purchased the land and gave it to the National Trust. The Trust whereupon reinstated the Coast Path. Did you find it that unsuitable?

Dartmouth – a bird's eye view.

7 Kingswear, Froward Point

Walks around water and woodland with wonderful views.

Considering how close is the big urban spread of Torbay this walk is remarkable for its tranquillity and lack of development. Inner Froward Point has the rare survival of a partly preserved site of a World War II coastal battery.

One section near the beginning does require care and there is a steep ascent later. However, you are rewarded with lovely views across the mouth of the River Dart and later out to sea.

Level 🐾 🐾 🐾 there is a difficult rocky descent and a particularly steep ascent.
Length three miles (4.6 km.)
Park at the National Trust Car Park Higher Brownstone Farm 905 509.
OS Map Explorer OL20 South Devon
Refreshments none so take your own.

Dartmouth Castle seen across the Dart.

Coleton Farm
Coleton Fishacre
▲ The Tower (Day Beacon)
Dartmouth Castle
Newfoundland Cove
Inner Froward Point
Outer Froward Point

1000 m

Plaque dedicated to Lt. Col H. Jones

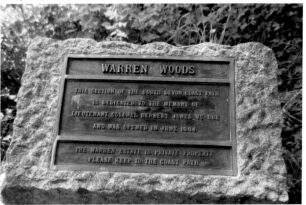

 Walk back out of the car park entrance but turn left, the road goes down to Higher Brownstone Farm. There are views forward across Start Bay to Start Point with its lighthouse. Take a right fork and pass through the sometimes busy farmyard. There are footpaths going left but ignore these. All the time follow the signs to 'Kingswear'.

2 There is then a steep rocky descent down a sunken footpath which is worn in places down to the bedrock. Care should be taken especially after heavy rain; the lower end of the route sometimes seems to prefer being a stream to a footpath!

3 At the bottom cross a little stream and go up the minor road. In season look for a show of colourful cyclamen in the roadside garden. Ignore the road coming in from the right and continue forward until you reach the top of the steps which are signed 'Coast Path'. Turn left down these.

At the top of the steps is a plaque in memory of Lt. Col H. Jones who won a Victoria Cross in the Falklands campaign in 1982.

4 Descend the wooden steps and then a steep footpath through the wood, at one point crossing over a another path. At the bottom there is a stile.

Believe it or not but the battlemented building just above the beach is a one-time water mill. Hence the beach was given the name of Mill Bay Cove.

5 Shortly after the stile there is a tee junction of paths, turn right and very soon turn left up a long ascent of made steps. As you near the top look for the wall pennywort beside the path. The path then takes a sinuous route through a wood to come out at high level above the River Dart.

Looking across the mouth of the river the big building on the hill opposite is the one time Coastguard Row at Little Dartmouth. The view also takes in Dartmouth Castle and the close by Church of St. Petrox. After a little while looking to your right can just be seen the corner of Kingswear Castle on this bank of the river. In early days, when invasion threatened, there was a chain between the two castles to prevent hostile ships entering the river mouth. Kingswear Castle was built in the late fifteenth century, at much the

A spectacular view towards Dartmouth and Kingswear.

Wall Pennywort.

same time as Dartmouth Castle. The tall conifers are Monterey Pines, an interesting Ice Age survivor originally found on just one peninsular in California. They were planted here in Devon at the beginning of the 20th century but suffered badly in the great gale of 1990. You can still see some of the fallen giants.

Wall Pennywort is also known as Navelwort, the former because of the round leaves about the size of an old penny the latter because of the dimple in the middle of the leaf. It grows in profusion in parts of the Westcountry but is not so common elsewhere.

6 The path continues through the wood then curving inwards and upwards behind Newfoundland Cove. It climbs, dips and climbs again to arrive at Inner Froward Point. Here the route leaves the Coast Path to follow the signs to 'Brownstone Car Park'. However, those that wish can explore the site of the Coastal Battery, descend alongside the miniature railway line that carried shells down to the guns and then further to the advanced searchlight post. This detour would however increase the distance of the walk.

The battery was constructed in 1942. It had six six-inch naval guns with a range of twenty miles. It was manned until 1945 but then 'mothballed' with a caretaker living on site. In 1956 coastal defences were disbanded and though most of the 'domestic' buildings have been demolished many of the operational ones remain. There is an information plaque and a small visitors' centre.

(7) The route inland passes through a gate and goes up between fields. There is the opportunity to take a cul-de-sac path to make a closer inspection of the Daymark. At each junction fork right to keep with the main track/roadway to arrive back at the car park. The long climb back to the car park can seem tedious, but when it does turn round and look at the superb view.

The Mewstone from Froward Point.

The Daymark is octopodial, in other words it has eight feet, it was built in 1864 as an aid to navigation and is eighty feet tall.

The octopodial Daymark.

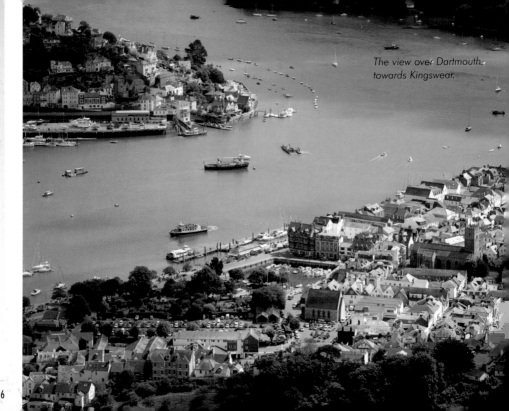

The view over Dartmouth towards Kingswear.

8 Teignmouth – Holcombe

Includes views of a famous railway alongside the sea.

Tame compared to much of the coast walking in this book but you will seldom walk so close to the sea. You will also be close to the famous railway line built by Brunel. It runs along beside the sea and gives every traveller to the Westcountry a first glimpse of seaside holidays.

A gentle walk in and close to an urban area.

The Salty forms a natural little harbour, with the houses of Teignmouth sitting alongside.

Holcombe

3

2

4 Hole Head

Sprey Point

1

Teignmouth

The Salty

The Point

1000 m

Level there is a climb near the start but by Coast Path standards it is mild.
Length about three and a half miles (5.6 km) but it does depend on where you have parked!
Park on Teignmouth sea front, some areas are free in winter.
OS Map Explorer 110 Torquay & Dawlish
Refreshments plentiful in Teignmouth.

Walk to the north-east end of the sea front where there is a turning circle. Here look at the sea if the tide is very high or there is a gale postpone the walk. From turning circle go slightly left up Eastcliffe Walk. Ignore minor turning forking left to cross railway bridge. Look inland at Catholic Church. At the end of the bridge go left into a park and follow the main gravel path uphill bearing mostly right. Ignore minor path going left to arrive in top corner of park where main path goes sharply left, here turn right to go through gap, turn left to proceed up stony track. Ignore footpath signed left; ignore another path signed right to go through a kissing gate still proceeding upwards. Note a large field gate on the right. The path eventually reaches tarmac

Teignmouth Catholic church.

where you need to bear left. After a short distance on tarmac roadway you

Palm trees winter wrapped at Teignmouth.

Teignmouth pier was built in 1865 was originally 700 feet long and had a ballroom added to the end in1890. It was shortened in the 1960s. • St Michael's church was originally Saxon and as late as 1763 was still thatched; unfortunately this interesting church was rebuilt by the Victorians. Cannonballs from a French raid in 1690 were found in the tower during reconstruction. • The Catholic Church was designed by an architect named Hansom, inventor of the cab of that name. • The large field gate mentioned in the text gives good views back to the Ness headland at Shaldon and along the coast to Hope's Nose at Torquay. Hope's Nose for a short while had a gold mine. It was never profitable but real gold was extracted.

reach the main Teignmouth – Dawlish road practically opposite an old toll-house.

2 Turn right on Teignmouth Road and cross when able. A little way down the hill, just

before an unusual thatched building called 'Minadab' turn left and take right fork at Holocene Road. The lane rises and when you are over the crest there are views forward across the mouth of the River Exe to Exmouth.

3 At the bottom of the hill turn right, Hall Lane, ignore left turn called The Orchard to come out again on the main road. Here cross

Holcombe, a mixture of old and new, was originally on the main road but is now a quiet backwater. The sea wall, a delight to walkers and railway photographers was built at the Admiralty's insistence. They required access to the foreshore when the railway was built. The line here was part of Brunel's projected Atmospheric Railway and in fact such trains ran for nearly a year but proved too expensive to operate commercially.

Seawall walk.

with care to go down Smugglers Lane. At the bottom go under the railway to climb steps and come out on the sea wall.

(4) Follow this all the way to Teignmouth, passing Sprey Point about half way along.

Parson and Clerk, now much eroded by the sea.

Sprey Point was formed by a cliff fall prior to building the railway in 1839. It had at one time a popular teahouse with outside table tennis and bagatelle. Stocks of refreshments and even a piano for entertainment were wheeled along the sea wall in a cart! • Offshore, just where the railway turns inland, is a mysterious wreck about 150 yards out. There is no record of a ship foundering here but from items recovered it was probably a Venetian vessel and possibly even a Spanish Armada supply ship. There is an information plaque about the wreck at the top of a few steps. Beside the notice can be seen a curved indentation in the red rock formed by an arch that once existed here made from the jaw bones of a whale!

Teignmouth looking up the Teign estuary.

9 Otterton Circuit

Walk in the footsteps of the Romans.

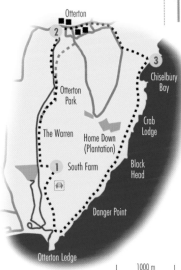

The part of the coast you walk is not as dramatic as many other stretches but is worth walking all the same.

Quite a lot of this walk is not on the coast but the long stretch alongside the River Otter is very pleasant. This makes for a generally easy walk in pleasant countryside

Level 🐾 🐾
Length six miles (9.6 km.)
Park by the verge on the east bank of the River Otter near Budleigh Salterton, close to the entrance of South Farm 076 831
OS Map Explorer 115 Exmouth & Sidmouth
Refreshments only in Otterton.

River Otter.

1000 m

53

① Walk back along the road crossing the bridge over the river to turn immediately right sign-posted 'Otterton 1½ miles'. Walk upstream alongside river, ignoring paths away from or across the river. When you reach the tarmac road at Otterton turn right crossing the bridge with care into the village.

Budleigh Salterton although it looks comparatively modern has a long history. The 'salt' in its name derives from the days long gone by when salt was extracted from seawater there. Strangers tend to shorten the town's name to 'Budleigh' the inhabitants on the other hand opt for 'Salterton'.
The River Otter rises in the Blackdown Hills just across the boundary in the next county Somerset. Appropriately the first significant place it passes in Devon is Upottery.

Poppies making a comeback.

View along the coast above Budleigh Salterton where the River Otter enters the sea.

Looking over Romano-British site towards Budleigh Salterton.

signed 'Ladram Bay', named Bell Street going uphill. Just after a 30-decontrol sign, fork right again and go over cross roads continuing up to Stantyway Farm a big building on right. Here turn left taking path signed 'To the Coast Path' that is tarmac as far as Monks Wall, a private house, here you leave the tarmac for a footpath. Follow this to the coast.

Otterton is a pleasant village with several cob (mixture of mud or clay mixed with straw) and thatched houses. It was once of more importance than it is today and had a priory but this was suppressed as early as 1414.

2 If you require refreshment Otterton is the only place on the circuit that provides it. Proceed along the main street, look for the attractive sign on the village green, then for a while there is a pleasant pavement walk between houses and stream. At the junction take right fork

3 Turn right on Coast Path sign-posted 'Budleigh Salterton'. The Coast Path continues to the mouth of the River Otter where you turn inland following well used path back to your parked car.

Where you turn inland and Otterton Ledge is offshore there is a large field. An ancient tile was found here a few years ago. A quick excavation was undertaken and a small Romano-British villa was revealed. There were two distinct buildings, one sparsely built probably used for farming and the other more substantial had a hypocaust for under-floor heating; just think of that nearly two thousand years ago!

View over the River Otter.

The remains of MSC Napoli.

10 Branscombe Mouth – Landslip

Shipwrecks, Sea Shanties and Landslips.

Landslips are a feature of the coastline in this area and make for a different kind of walking. Sometimes the paths can be very sinuous and undulating at the same time.

This walk is a chance to sample undercliff or landslip walking but there is an over 400 ft steep climb at the start!

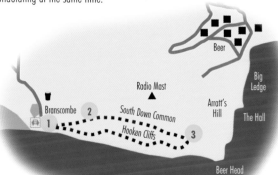

1000 m

Level 🥾🥾
Length only two and a half miles (4 km) but remember the hill!
Park the car park at Branscombe Mouth 207 882
OS Maps the start is on Explorer 115 Exmouth & Sidmouth, the remainder is on Explorer 111 Lyme Regis & Bridport
Refreshments there is a large café at Branscombe mouth.

Beer Head looking towards Seaton.

① Cross the road by the water splash to take the path up the hill National Trust East Cliff, signposted 'Coast Path Beer'. Shortly the Coast Path goes right but keep on up the hill to the left signposted 'Hooken Cliff ½ mile' eventually reaching the top.

Branscombe was once owned by King Alfred the Saxon king. • The Sea Shanty Café was formerly a coal yard mostly used for storage for local limekilns. • Not so long ago a local occupation was collecting round pebbles off the beach. These were put into sacks and sent away to be used in ball mills to grind materials, such as pottery colourings into fine powder. • Today Branscombe is chiefly remembered for the wreck of the MSC Napoli in 2007 the remains of which can still be seen.

Hooken Cliffs, pillars resultant of landslip action.

Branscombe Mouth.

(2) At the top go forward keeping near the cliff top. Presently you pass a watch house and still keep by the cliff to go through a gap of an old hedge and very soon, a kissing gate. Now be sure you keep with cliff edge, a broad path goes slightly left but it is NOT what you want. Continuing with cliff edge you descend into a dip where you turn back right on to the Coast Path signposted, 'Branscombe Mouth'. (You can extend your walk by half a mile if you go forward to Beer Head to get a view of Seaton before you descend to the landslip).

The watch tower was once a coastguard lookout. • There are two suggested origins of the term kissing gate - the mundane and the romantic. The mundane is that the gate just touches or kisses its frame on either side. The romantic is that the young man can exact a toll of a kiss from the young lady before he releases the gate to let her through! • The cliffs here are made of chalk and are the most westerly ones on the South coast of England, a long way indeed from the better known White Cliffs at Dover.

Near the tunnel entrance on Hooken Cliff.

The beach at Branscombe, with Seaton visible in the distance.

You then descend into landslip or undercliff area. Presently observe an oblong opening high up on the cliff face behind you. Later there are one or two paths going down to beach but keep on through the landslip area. If it is autumn look for the attractive spindle trees. The last few yards become a track through a chalet area but you soon cross a cattle grid to descend again to Branscombe Mouth.

Above: Spindle berries in Landslip

This area is well known for its landslips the biggest being between Axmouth and Lyme Regis somewhat east of here. This one though, near Branscombe, predates that one by about fifty years having occurred in 1791. • The oblong opening in the cliffs is not a cave but a man-made tunnel. The Beer stone here, was much used in church interiors, and was quarried and shaped underground whilst it was still relatively soft. After it was exposed to the air for a while it hardened and became a fine building stone. • Spindle trees are so called because their wood was used to make spindles. It was also used to make wooden skewers.